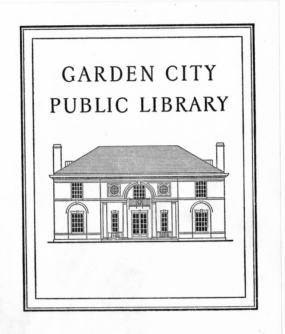

The Wonders of Algae

THE WONDERS
OF ALGAE

LUCY KAVALER

Illustrated with photographs
and with drawings by
BARBARA AMLICK and RICHARD OTT

THE JOHN DAY COMPANY
NEW YORK

Library of Congress Catalogue Card Number: 61-8281

Manufactured in the United States of America

Third Impression

To My Mother and Father

CONTENTS

The Wonders of Algae

1·

LET'S TAKE A LOOK AT ALGAE

WHEN YOU SEE the green slime on the glass sides of your fish tank, you'd never think that what you're looking at may some day keep men alive in outer space.

The oxygen the interplanetary travelers will breathe will be given to them by the tiny plants that make up the green slime in your fish tank, the scum on the top of stagnant ponds and the film that you find on the bark of trees.

The name of this group of plants is algae. You pronounce the word as if it were spelled "AL-jee." These plants are the simplest form of life on earth. Many kinds of algae have only one cell — no root, no stem, no leaves and no flowers.

But it is their very simplicity that makes them ideally suited for use on spaceships. All they need to make them grow is water, light, the carbon dioxide breathed out by the space pilots and the nitrogen and other minerals that

11

can be gotten from the men's daily wastes. Algae grow with incredible speed, so that a small cargo could continue to produce oxygen all the way to Mars and back.

As a side benefit, these one-celled plants can be used as food. A dish of algae doesn't have to look like green slime or taste like it, either. When the pilot and crew sit down to dinner in their spaceship, they will find that the slime has been changed as if by magic into a tasty meal. And a wholesome one, too. A diet of algae alone provides all the vitamins, minerals, protein, fats and starches that you get in a full-course dinner of roast beef, French fries, string beans, peaches and cookies.

These plants are so healthful that you may find yourself eating algae one day, even if you don't make your way to Saturn or Pluto. Scientists are working on ways of getting them onto dinner tables on earth, as well as in outer space.

The idea of using algae to provide food and oxygen on rocket ships is new, of course. But algae are not new. They are the oldest form of life we know.

Have you ever wished that you could go back through time and see the world as it was when it was young? It was very still then and very strange . . . long before man appeared, before the ape, even before the dinosaur, the saber-toothed tiger and the woolly mammoth. There were no trees or flowers or creeping vines. You would have seen only the earth beneath your feet, and the rocks, only water and sky. And yet on that long-ago day, you would have seen one living thing that has come down through the ages almost unchanged. Just as you might today, you would have seen algae, clinging like a green shadow to the prehistoric rock.

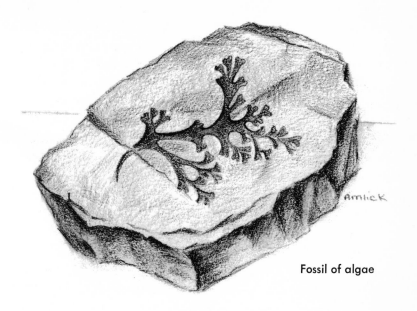

Fossil of algae

How do we know this? Only a few years ago, two scientists were searching for fossils, the remains of prehistoric life. They found some flint rock in an ancient iron deposit. This rock turned out to be one of the oldest in the world, more than two billion years old. You can imagine the men's surprise when they discovered fossils of algae lying deep within the rock. The scientists realized that they were looking at the oldest organisms ever seen by man.

It was like seeing the beginning of history. The plants we know today are descendants of those early algae. The theory of evolution is just as true for plant life as it is for animals and for man. Through the ages, plants became more and more complicated.

You've never seen a real live Neanderthal man. And you're never going to. Those prehistoric apelike cavemen vanished thousands and thousands of years ago, replaced by men of a more highly developed intelligence. The prehistoric plants that fed and sheltered them have changed, too, beyond recognition. But evolution has passed one of them by. You can look at living plants today that are exactly the way they were billions of years ago. The two-billion-year-old fossils and the slime on the sides of your fish tank are just the same.

There are many different kinds of algae. But the ones that will play the biggest part in the world of the future are the most primitive and the simplest. They are smaller than the tiniest thing you can imagine. It takes billions and trillions of them to cover the glass on just one side of your fish tank. You could fit a thousand of them on the head of a pin. But numbers mean nothing to algae. They multiply much faster than rabbits. But then, why shouldn't they? All they need to do to reproduce is to split in half, and they do this every few hours. That is why they can cover the side of your fish tank so quickly.

Not all algae are as simple as these. Through the ages, a number of these plants did reach a slightly higher stage of development. Some algae are big, stretching out for one hundred or even two hundred feet. This does not mean that the single cell is so big. The way it works is that a lot of cells are strung together in colonies or ribbons. Sometimes they look like leaves, but study under a microscope has shown that they are not true leaves. They are simply repetitions of the same cells.

You have run across some of the bigger algae hundreds of times, though you may not have realized that they were algae, too. You probably called them by another name: "seaweed." Actually, "seaweed" is not another name at

Marine algae

Amlick

all. It is simply the English translation of the Latin word *alga* (or *algae,* which is the plural). That is the name the Romans gave to seaweed. The ancients did not have microscopes to study cell structure. They did not know that there were smaller plants belonging to the same family. That was discovered much later. And the whole family adopted the name of its largest child.

It is a family with an unbelievably large number of sisters and cousins and aunts. Some scientists say that there are 10,000 species or types of algae. Others argue that this figure is too small; there are really 17,000. And there is a group that insists on numbering 20,000 species as algae. Whatever you believe, one thing is clear: There are a great many kinds of algae. And each type is slightly different from all the others.

They come in a number of colors, too: green, blue-green, red and brown. The ones you see most often are either green or blue-green. These algae usually grow in fresh-water ponds, in shallow parts of the ocean, on trees, in the soil and on rocks. The red algae are most often found in the lower depths of the ocean. The deeper you go, the darker the color. In some places, these plants are actually purple. Red algae are also found in pools where overhanging rocks shield them from the sun. The brown algae are most often seen along the shore where they are exposed to the sun at low tide and then covered with water when the tide comes in.

You'll find some form of algae wherever you go in the whole world. The Russians have them. So do the Indians, the Fiji Islanders and the Eskimos. Join the next Antarctic expedition. You'll find red algae there, giving a pink glow to the glacial ice. Take a trip to the tropics. Algae are float-

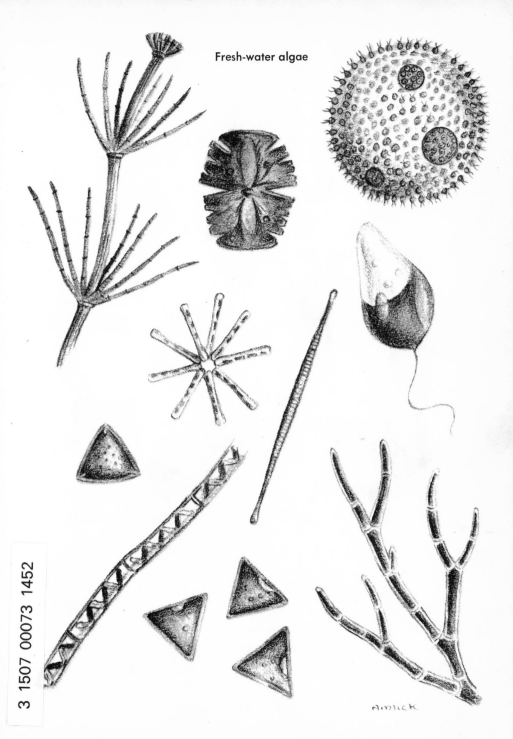

Fresh-water algae

ing in the warm waters. Some form of algae can exist in all climates, in fresh or salt water and in the soil.

Thousands of years ago men discovered that algae had many wonderful uses. They did not suspect the exciting possibilities of the one-celled algae. They did not even know of them. The only algae they recognized were the seaweeds. But they knew that seaweed was valuable.

Some primitive peoples were afraid of it. The ancient Scandinavians were certain that seaweed was bewitched. Sorcerers used it in weaving magic spells.

But in most other civilizations, more commonplace uses were found for algae. Throughout the Far East, seaweed was dried and eaten. The idea may not appeal to you, but the ancient Chinese thought as much of seaweed as we do of steak or chocolate layer cake. That odd fact was revealed in a book of Chinese poetry written by a forgotten poet more than 2,600 years ago. The poet told about a young woman preparing a sacrifice for her ancestors. It was the custom in those days to offer the most wonderful foods to do honor to the dead. The young woman, therefore, presented boiled algae as her gift to her forefathers.

Seaweed has been used as a medicine since the dawn of that science. More than five thousand years ago, a great Chinese doctor named Shen Nung recommended the weed to his patients. He was the first we know of, but as we trace the history of medicine in one country after another, we find that algae have been used to treat disease. Seaweed was prescribed for stomach disorders, goiters, abscesses, lung conditions and dropsy. The ancient Polynesians used one type of algae to make poultices for sore eyes and found another that worked as a laxative.

Coming down to more recent times, the monks in the Middle Ages considered algae an excellent stomach remedy. They were careful to change the taste. The weed was boiled into a jelly and then ginger and sugar were sprinkled over it. The monks also made a milk paste out of the algae. This was served with sugar and vinegar. The men liked the flavor and believed the paste would protect them from heat prostration.

Modern doctors do not laugh at these primitive remedies. They have found that many times men stumbled by chance on the right way of treating an illness. Today we know why seaweed was effective in soothing stomach-aches. Agar-agar, which comes from seaweed, is a very good laxative. The primitive idea of treating goiters with a seaweed medicine was surprisingly sound. Goiter, a swelling of the neck, is caused by a lack of iodine in the body, and is controlled today by heavy doses of iodine. Seaweed, we have learned, is very high in iodine. As for our monks and their milk paste, that was not such a bad idea either. You may sometimes have been given salt pills to prevent you from feeling sick in very hot weather. Seaweed is full of salt.

Since time immemorial, seaweed has been used to improve the soil. Modern agricultural experts again back up the judgment of the unschooled farmers of ancient days. Laboratory research reveals that the minerals in algae are very much like those put into the best artificial fertilizers.

Guided by nothing but instinct, natives of certain Pacific islands for generations covered fish with seaweed. When they did this, they found the fish stayed fresh longer. It is only recently that scientists discovered that seaweed has antibiotics in it, and that antibiotics keep food from spoiling. Today the food processing industry in America is beginning to follow that very principle.

In some countries, algae's color was put to use. In ancient Rome, material for clothing was dyed purple with a dye made from the darkest of the seaweed. The Roman ladies of that era were every bit as beauty-conscious as women are today. They added a faint glow to their complexions with a rouge made from red algae.

Eskimo women formerly did the same thing, mixing fish oil with a red dye from seaweed to add color to their faces. And Eskimos found a use for another form of the weed: they made it into an alcoholic beverage.

As science has advanced, more uses have been found for the large algae. They've been put in foods that you eat regularly — and that don't look the least bit like seaweed. Puddings jell because of a product gotten from seaweed. Ice cream and chocolate milk are thickened by a similar product. The casings on frankfurters and sausages are part seaweed, too.

All these uses are important. But they are a mere drop in the bucket when you think that algae can provide oxygen and food for men in spaceships and in atomic submarines as well. They can even supply food for the hungry all over the world.

2.

THE SPACE AGE

THE SPACE AGE is here. Men are preparing to travel beyond the earth's atmosphere, to visit planets and to lay bare many of the secrets of the universe.

You have probably imagined yourself as a space traveler, seen yourself discovering the truth about the craters of the moon, or whether there really is life on Mars. But have you ever considered the practical side of such a trip? Scientists figure that a rocket ship would get to Mars in 138 days. You would need to stay there a while to explore. Then would come the trip back. It takes longer to return from Mars than to go there . . . just about 175 days.

But, of course, you would not limit yourself to Mars. The more distant planets beckon, too. Venus, for instance, is 295 days away. The voyage back in this case is shorter — but it still would take about 223 days.

If you were one of the crew of the Mars or Venus

The atomic submarine the U.S.S. *Nautilus* under way

project, how would you get the oxygen to breathe? You couldn't take along enough in tanks to last more than five hundred days on the round trip to Venus or even the three hundred plus for Mars. How would you get rid of the carbon dioxide you breathed out? You couldn't just open a window in outer space. And unless some way could be found to clear the air, you would suffocate.

Not long ago a group of scientists working for the Air Force and the Navy Department met to discuss the physiological side of space travel and also of underwater exploration. The problems facing the designers of nuclear submarines are just about the same as for spaceships. Men on these submarines are also out of the earth's atmosphere for long periods of time. Tons of water separate them from the life-giving air. So far atomic submarine trips have been comparatively short, and oxygen has been taken along. But long periods of underwater exploration are being planned.

"What we need is something that works just like a living green plant — taking in carbon dioxide and giving out oxygen over and over again," stated one biologist. "Somehow science has never been able to come up with a substitute."

The system this scientist was referring to is known as photosynthesis. It is the process whereby green plants absorb water and carbon dioxide and use them to form starches and sugars. This is how plants grow. During the change, oxygen is released. The whole process is triggered by light. That is why you must always keep potted plants near a window.

Photosynthesis was first observed in the late eighteenth century by a great English scientist named Joseph Priestley. He put a mouse in one big bell jar and a geranium in another, and connected the two containers with a glass tube. So long as the plant was exposed to light, both the mouse and the geranium thrived. When the light was removed, they died. The reason, we know now, is that without light, photosynthesis did not take place. The plant could not absorb the carbon dioxide and use it to make oxygen for the mouse. If the duct between the two jars were to be closed, both plant and animal would die, too, even if the light were still there. They depend upon one another for life.

If you have a fish tank, you see this principle at work every day. Perhaps you never fully realized why you were told to put some plants in your aquarium and to keep it near a window or attach a small electric light to the rim. Many people think that greenery is placed in a tank for decoration only. It is actually essential to the life of the fish. They take in oxygen from water and return carbon dioxide to it, much as we do in the air. Underwater plants take in this carbon dioxide and replace it with oxygen. When this process is working, scientists say that you have a "balanced aquarium."

It is this principle that must in some way be applied to spaceships and nuclear submarines.

"If nothing works as well as a green plant, we must take one along?" That was the conclusion reached by the scientists.

Obviously, a spaceship could not be filled with huge potted geraniums or calla lilies. To be suitable, a plant would have to be small, require little care and reproduce rapidly. And this is where the one-celled algae come in. Scientists have long known that these microscopic plants are better at turning carbon dioxide and water into oxygen and food than are more complicated plants. Algae have been used for laboratory studies of the way photosynthesis works for over thirty years.

But size and efficiency are not the only things algae have to recommend them.

"An extra advantage of using algae is that they can absorb human wastes," added another of the biologists at the meeting. "And that is a real problem on board spaceships."

In order to grow, algae need not only carbon dioxide, but also water containing nitrogen, magnesium, phosphorus, potassium and other chemicals. Practically all of these are present in the products of human digestion and excretion. If these wastes are fed to the algae, they will be used up in the photosynthetic process. When it is over, the algae will have transformed the wastes into valuable oxygen and carbohydrates, which is the scientific name for starches and sugars. These carbohydrates can then be made into food. That is yet another advantage of sending algae into outer space.

By changing the proportions of the carbon dioxide and minerals given the algae, the amount of carbohydrates, fats and protein in the cells can be varied. This is important when only one source of food is taken along. Fat algae can be developed to provide the nourishment of butter and high-protein algae to substitute for meat.

You can easily see why the scientists became so excited about the possibilities of using algae. This one plant can solve all of the most pressing physical problems of space travelers.

And so Operation Algae got under way. It quickly became clear to the scientists that the key to the success of any apparatus they might design lay in the selection of the right kind of algae. Not all of the 10,000 or more species of the plant are efficient. Some can grow only at low temperatures; others reproduce very slowly. There are even types in which the cells cling together to form huge colonies. And a number of algae have a repulsive smell.

After months of research, the men decided that the most suitable algae belonged to a group with the pretty name of Chlorella. These one-celled green algae are exceptionally high in protein. They can be processed into good and nourishing food, and they reproduce by splitting in half and separating.

But even among the Chlorella, there are many variations. For a long time, biologists experimented with one type which grows best at room temperature. But gradually they were forced to the realization that it simply wouldn't

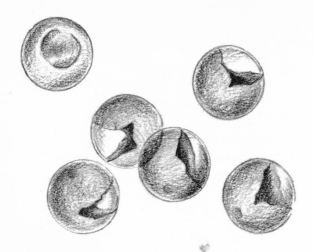

Cells of Chlorella greatly magnified

work in outer space. As soon as the thermometer rose above 85°F., this Chlorella stopped growing altogether. And as the algae must be exposed to sunlight or brilliant artificial light, the temperature around the tank is usually higher than that. In order to keep the Chlorella in good condition, it had to be cooled. And cooling machinery is both expensive and heavy — a serious matter in a spaceship where ounces are counted.

As the scientists checked the algae tanks, they realized that this strain reproduced too slowly. This is more important than it seems at first. The slower plants grow, the less oxygen they have to offer spacemen. Several biologists measured the amount of oxygen given off by these Chlorella. They discovered that 110 gallons of water with algae in it would be needed to provide oxygen for a single man.

The hot plains of Texas

The equipment would occupy at best 20 cubic feet per man, and possibly as much as 100. At this point, they were ready to give way to despair. With all that algae, there would be no room on board for other equipment.

The scientists became explorers, going on journeys to far-off places in search of the perfect Chlorella. One Air Force biologist had a float plane land him on Schrader Lake, a body of water hidden among the mountain ranges of Alaska. There he gathered specimens of algae and took them back to be studied at the School of Aviation Medicine at Randolph Air Force Base in Texas. At the same time, a park warden at Yellowstone National Park in Wyoming was asked to collect algae there and send them along to the school. Other men were searching the hot plains of Texas.

And at last success came when two scientists discovered a new strain of Chlorella in Texas. One of them was an American, Jack Myers of the Department of Zoology at the University of Texas. He is one of the world's leading algologists — that's what scientists who specialize in algae are called. The other, Constantine Sorokin, is a former Russian scientist who was captured by the Germans during World War II. After the war, instead of returning to the U.S.S.R., he came to the United States. And that is how we have the benefit of his discovery.

What can this strain of Chlorella do that the others can't? In the first place, it likes to be hot. These algae are happiest when the thermometer hovers around 105°F. In addition, they reproduce at staggering speed. It takes only two and one-half hours for them to double their dry weight. As that doubled weight doubles itself in another two and one-half hours, you can see that one tiny Chlorella plant can quickly become a multitude. In the course of a single day and night, each plant can produce one thousand new ones!

This sounds like an exaggeration, but many scientists think it is too modest a claim. In some experiments, the reproduction time has been speeded up to two hours. When that happens, each plant becomes the ancestor of 10,000 new ones in twenty-four hours.

This incredible rate of growth changed all the calculations. The biologists again took out pencil and paper to figure out how much algae would be needed to sustain a crew in a spaceship or nuclear submarine. And they found that equipment using this strain of Chlorella would take up only three to five cubic feet of space per man. As a spaceship that requires a crew of only eight men has already been designed, you can see that enough algae to serve them would not weigh the ship down too much.

The biologists then made another discovery about this miraculous one-celled plant. The amount of algae needed to produce enough oxygen to keep one man alive will provide the exact quantity of food he needs, too.

The discovery of the suitable form of algae was only the beginning. Scientists and engineers had to join forces to design the machinery to be used . . . to make it possible for algae to bring oxygen and food to the far reaches of the universe.

3·

THE ALGAE MACHINE

HOW COULD the wonderful newly discovered strain of algae be put to work? scientists asked one another.

"The little plants can hardly be left on the loose floating around the spaceship," joked one. "We'll have to make an algae machine."

After long months of effort, a machine was developed and given the impressive name of "photosynthetic gas exchanger." If you take that name a little at a time, you can see that it describes exactly what the apparatus must do. By using the process of photosynthesis, it exchanges one gas — carbon dioxide — for another — oxygen.

The largest part of the gas exchanger is the glass tank containing the algae suspension. The word "suspension" means that the algae cells are in a liquid but do not dissolve. They float in it, instead. The correct term for the liquid is a "culture medium." In this case, it contains

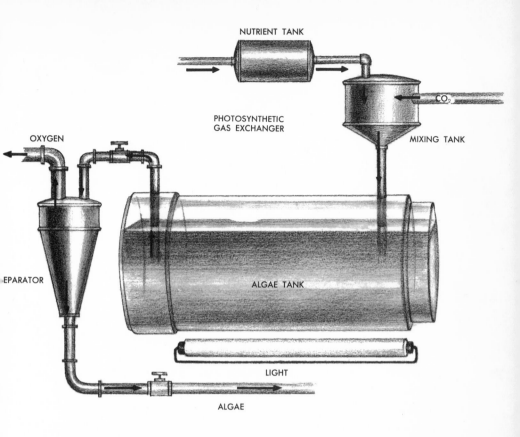

water, carbon dioxide and the chemical ingredients needed to make the algae grow.

"Just about everything connected with space travel is fabulously expensive," comments an Air Force officer, "except for algae. A test tube containing enough algae to start an entire spaceship system can be bought for just about a dollar."

The life-giving tank is no bigger than an elongated bongo drum. The carbon dioxide that nourishes the algae is brought in by a tube hooked up with the exhaust system of the spaceship or submarine. The chemicals are taken from human wastes. The urine is filtered through charcoal

31

to remove its color and odor before being added to the liquid. Feces are burned, and only the ashes are put into the suspension. The algae, just to make it a perfect circle, provide the oxygen for burning the wastes.

You surely take light for granted in much the same way as water or air. On spaceships you could continue to do that. The plan is to put the algae equipment at the very top of the rocket ship. This is the part of the ship where the crew would live. It is to contain bedrooms, bathrooms, galleys, game rooms and a gymnasium, a library, medical room, storage room and equipment — including the photosynthetic gas exchanger. The rays of the sun would light this section.

"On submarines, however, it is quite a different story," say officials of the Navy Department. "No ray of light can filter through the heavy ocean waves beneath which the nuclear ship is traveling. And so we have to use brilliant artificial lights for our algae."

This is, oddly enough, a major problem. Standard incandescent light bulbs last only about 200 hours. That's long enough when you can run over to the supermarket and buy some more. But a submarine is cut off from the world above. You have to take along whatever you're going to need. Very little space can be allowed for stocks of extra light bulbs to illuminate the gas exchanger. Algae do not require constant lighting. In fact, many scientists believe that they grow best when light is turned on and off. But even so, they would need a tremendous number of light bulbs during a long voyage.

"What we need," said the men planning the atomic submarine program, "is a new type of bulb that can burn for three months or more. It must be tiny. And it should be extremely bright."

That sounds like a tall order. But the research men were not dismayed. A bulb was developed by the General Electric Co. that has a life of between 2,000 and 5,000 hours. It burns with a light five to ten times brighter than sunlight. And it is very small. The new bulb is just about the size of a pencil — nine inches long and ⅜ of an inch in diameter. You can see that a cargo of replacements would take up very little space on board.

The engineers seized these new bulbs and fitted them into working models of the photosynthetic gas exchangers. They found that six of these bulbs provided all the light needed for photosynthesis.

The algae are pumped past the light. It is essential, by the way, to keep the mixture moving; otherwise, the plants grow more slowly. As photosynthesis takes place, oxygen is released. A tube takes the gas from the tank and lets it out in the cabin of the ship.

While this is going on, the Chlorella go on splitting in two as fast as they can. As you might imagine, this can get to be too much of a good thing. When the tank gets over-crowded, the algae stop growing . . . and no growth, no oxygen. The number of algae must be kept under control.

"The liquid should be just about the thickness of blood — bright green blood," explains an algologist.

As is the way of the world, young cells grow better than do old ones. And so a system was worked out to draw the tired, spent algae cells out of the tank through a tube. And these serve a purpose, too — a most important one. They are the cells that can be dried, processed and used as food.

This idea appeals more to the Air Force than it does to the Navy. The Navy Department concentrates on algae's role as an oxygen producer only.

"It's hard to turn algae into good food," comments a scientist at a nuclear submarine base. "On spaceships, it may be necessary to do that. The crew can't pack enough food concentrates to last indefinitely. And there's no way for them to get rid of the extra algae. They can't just throw it out of the spaceship. Without gravity, it would come right back and hit them. They've got to like algae or lump it.

"Our problem is quite different. We can take enough food concentrates to last for months undersea. The leftover algae can be dumped overboard. We only need algae to provide us with oxygen and to keep the air free of carbon dioxide."

Air Force scientists must worry about water as well as food. Submarines can carry quite a lot of liquid. When they run out, the crew can take in sea water and purify it. But space travelers must find a way of making their own water. So far no one has been able to come up with any continuing source besides urine. This can be filtered and treated until it is transformed into water that is just like any other in terms of purity, taste and color. The algae must drink this, too. Their needs are small, as they can use the same liquid over and over again. But even so they must be given some fresh water every now and again. And so the scientists planning the size of the equipment that will turn urine or sea water into fresh water must figure in the needs of the algae in the photosynthetic gas exchanger.

"It will be worth it, because the exchanger can support any number of men," reports a biologist at the Electric Boat Division of the General Dynamics Corp. "It is simply a question of engineering. We believe that our working models of the exchanger can provide food and oxygen for four men. Now if a system can support four men, it can support fifty, or one hundred, for that matter. It depends on the intensity of the light and the amount of algae in the culture. All we need to do is make a bigger machine with more light bulbs and a larger algae tank."

The scientist was talking about theories. And all the evidence certainly indicated that the gas exchanger would work. But theories are not enough. Once a spaceship was halfway to the moon, it would be too late to discover that some detail had been overlooked.

Modern medicine admits its debt to such small animals as the guinea pig and the rat. Men in space may have to express their gratitude to the humble mouse. These little rodents were the first living creatures to risk their lives in the photosynthetic gas exchanger.

Four mice were placed in a sealed chamber. The exchanger was their only source of oxygen. It was also the only way provided to clear the air of the carbon dioxide they breathed out. The mice stayed in the chamber for fifteen days and then scampered out hale and hearty.

The next step was to see whether a bigger animal could survive under these conditions. And so monkeys took their turn in the preparations for man's conquest of outer space. For the first test, a monkey was strapped in a chair with only its arms free. This chair was then placed in a sealed chamber with transparent plastic covering the ends. One tube brought the oxygen in from the algae tank; another carried the carbon dioxide out to the tank.

For the first experiment, the monkey was left in his prison for only two and a half hours. If monkeys could talk, he would no doubt have said that it seemed like a year.

In later experiments, monkeys were kept in the sealed chamber for as long as thirty days — with no ill effects.

The ultimate test of the gas exchanger must be made with human beings. This dress rehearsal will be performed on solid ground, not in outer space, to be sure.

Civil defense officials are very much interested in the photosynthetic gas exchanger, too. There is yet another possible future use for algae. We don't like to think about it, and yet we can't overlook it. The exchangers may be needed in fallout shelters. Algae would make it possible for people to survive for weeks and months in a chamber sealed to keep out radioactivity.

"At present, the difficulty and expense of making the apparatus are so great that we cannot consider mass production," say officials. "But a few exchangers might be prepared to protect men who are essential to the winning of a war."

In time, improvements in engineering and design and discovery of cheaper sources of light and even more efficient strains of algae would make it possible for the machines to be more widely used.

But the main future for the exchanger, we must hope, will be in helping man to push back the frontiers of the universe. Rocket ships are only the beginning of our space projects. There are plans also to place satellites with men on them in orbit. These satellites could be supplied with gas exchangers.

"We don't need to limit ourselves to brief journeys of exploration," say government officials. "Men could actually live on other planets for extended periods of time. They could then conduct really long-range experiments."

Where would they live? In houses, of course. Scientists are working on blueprints for houses which could be built on distant planets. The materials would be carried on the spaceships. The houses would be quite different from the ones you are used to. The windows — if there were any — would let in light, but they would be sealed tight. The earthmen, whose lungs are not designed for life on other planets, would take their oxygen from a photosynthetic gas exchanger. Their homes would be a sealed chamber. It is strange to realize that the day may come when algae will support life on planets yet unknown.

"Algae might even provide the seeds from which life could develop on planets that are now dead," say a number of astronomers.

The earthmen could leave algae and microbes on the barren ground of other worlds. Higher forms of life might gradually evolve from them. And maybe in a billion years there would be intelligent creatures on those planets — if there are not already.

Thomas Gold, a well-known astronomer, has suggested that life on the earth may have started in just this way. Perhaps billions of years ago, space travelers from other more highly developed planets landed here, leaving algae behind as they departed.

No one can say that this is true. But no one can be sure that it isn't.

This is just one more example of the limitless possibilities in the single cell of the simplest and oldest plant known to man.

4.

PRETTY GREEN FOOD

ONE AFTERNOON not too long ago, a number of scientists at the Carnegie Institute in California were pleased to receive an invitation to tea from Dr. Hirosi Tamiya, a visiting Japanese scientist. With enjoyment, they ate what amounted to a regular meal, with soup, noodles, rolls, tea and a dessert of ice cream. Some of them were a little startled by the rolls, which seemed to be more suitable for a Saint Patrick's Day party than a gathering of serious-minded scientists. They were a pretty pale green color. Perhaps you have already guessed the reason. The rolls were made with algae. So were the soup, the noodles, the tea, and even the ice cream. Dr. Tamiya was trying to prove that algae can taste good.

It's particularly important for algae to taste good, be-cause they are so good for you. A single tablespoonful of Chlorella has as much food value as an ounce of steak. Its

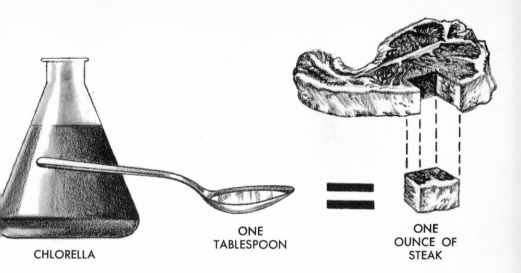

CHLORELLA   ONE TABLESPOON = ONE OUNCE OF STEAK

one cell is like a treasure chest with unbelievable riches inside. The treasure is not made up of gold or jewels. It is even more valuable in terms of human life. Chlorella is over half protein, the energy supply you find in meat.

You'd need to count the vitamins listed on the label of your bottle of multi-vitamin capsules to know how many vitamins are stored in the algae cell. The only one missing is vitamin C. And there are bonuses of fats and starches. If you were going to live on only one kind of food, you wouldn't be badly off if you picked algae. Quite an accomplishment for a plant with only one cell, isn't it?

When scientists became aware of the nutritional value of algae, their first idea was to use it as animal feed. Animals are not so fussy about taste or smell. And they could benefit from the vitamins and proteins. Rats and chickens got the first chance at the algae diets. Most of them liked the new food and thrived on it. Now farmers are considering it for pigs.

But what it can do for animals led many to wonder

what it would do for human beings. At the Cabo Blanco Leprosarium in Venezuela, many of the lepers were suffering from malnutrition. Their doctor, Jorgen Jorgensen, racked his brains to find some way of improving their diets. At last he got an idea. He gathered algae from local mudholes and water tanks and placed them in a liquid containing some chemicals and water taken from the neighboring town of Maiquetia. In Maiquetia, the water is not treated in any way that would kill algae and other organisms. Dr. Jorgensen thought that was so much the better, as algae were just what he wanted.

The one-celled plants were placed in bowls made of unglazed baked red clay and exposed to the brilliant tropical sun. The result was a kind of thick algal soup. This was boiled for about twenty minutes, and a little salt was added to it. That was all. Then it was given to the patients at the leprosarium. Most of the lepers who ate the soup felt better for it. They had more energy and even gained weight.

The lepers wanted to get better, and so were ready to try anything, no matter what it looked or tasted like. But we insist on food that tastes good, looks good and smells good. In their natural form, the one-celled plants do not live up to a single one of these requirements.

What is the flavor like? It's something like dried lima beans. You could manage to eat plain algae if you had to, but you'd hardly beg for a second helping. The color is a particularly intense shade of dark green. And the smell is grassy. It's not horrible, but you don't think of grass as something to eat. And all of us want to eat food that smells like food.

Scientists found that by treating the algae with alcohol, some of the color could be removed. The plants were still green, but a softer, pleasanter shade. Algae can also be bleached under brilliant fluorescent lights. Bleaching algae has several advantages, in addition to improving the color. The smell becomes milder, and so does the taste.

A lot more can be done to mask the natural flavor of algae. Artificial flavors are made today that can fool a panel of experts. Look at the label on the next candy bar you eat. In small print, you'll see the words "artificial flavoring." Go through the cookie shelves at the supermarket and try to find even one box that does not contain artificial flavoring. You probably couldn't tell if the chocolate cake you eat is made of real chocolate or of laboratory chocolate and brown food coloring. Vanilla ice cream has just a drop of natural vanilla in it; most of the flavor is synthetic. Many small children eat medicine as if it were candy. Artificial flavoring produces that magic. These man-made flavors are not just for sweets, either. Almost any taste that exists in nature can be reproduced in the laboratory — from pepper to mushroom to beef to fish.

That's why flavor chemists insist that you can forget the way algae taste in their natural form. By the time you pop a slice of algal bread into the toaster, you can be sure that it will taste like bread — and good bread at that.

Chances are that you wouldn't be eating plain algae anyway. The idea is to add some of it to other foods — a pinch here, a dash there, a cupful somewhere else. Foods that are not healthful in themselves can be greatly improved by the addition of algae. Lots of people like tea, but no one has ever claimed it was nourishing. When algae are added, tea can become as health-giving as concentrated beef broth. Chicken soup is even better for you when algae are added. And quite a lot can be slipped into bread without affecting the taste.

41

We usually think of the French as being the world's best cooks. But when it comes to algae, they don't hold a candle to the Japanese. In that Far Eastern country, nutrition experts have worked out recipes using algae for all types of dishes from meat balls to stuffed eggs. If you like to eat in Chinese restaurants, you know what soy sauce is. It's a favorite seasoning in Japan, too. And the Japanese have worked out a way of making soy sauce out of algae.

In order to cook with algae, a number of scientists at the Tokugawa Institute for Biological Research in Tokyo grew some Chlorella in a culture medium. Then they separated the algae from the liquid by spinning it in a machine called a centrifuge. They washed the plants once or twice. The next step was to dry them. For this they used infrared lamps and a plain old-fashioned electric fan. They discovered that algae dried at temperatures lower than 59°F. had a milder taste and smell than those dried at higher temperatures. The dried cells were then crushed and ground to powder in a mortar. And the algal powder joined the flour, milk, eggs and other ingredients listed in standard recipes.

Perhaps that sounds like a lot of trouble to you, but it certainly doesn't compare with the difficulty of getting corn flakes out of an ear of corn, or making shredded wheat. Huge factories have been built to get these staples to your breakfast table. And everybody takes dried cereal as a matter of course. The same thing could happen to algae.

As tea is the most popular drink in the Far East, the Japanese cooks started out by seeing how much algae could be added without changing the taste. After all, no one will drink tea that tastes like lima beans. And they found that they could slip in one spoonful of powdered algae along

42

Tokugawa Institute for Biological Research

Some foods prepared with Chlorella as an ingredient:

noodles   soup   cookies

candies   jelly roll

with four spoonfuls of green tea . . . and no one was the wiser.

Then they tried adding a couple of spoonfuls of Chlorella to bean, mushroom, beef, and chicken soup and consommé. The algae were most suitable for cream soups. Clear soups ended up a bright green.

Knowing that the Italians consider green noodles a delicacy, the chefs decided that algae's natural color would be no drawback there. And sure enough, green algal noodles proved to be a carbon copy of the original.

To everyone's surprise, algae ice cream was delicious. Green ice cream isn't startling anyway — pistachio is a standard popular flavor all over the United States. The algae actually bring out almost any ice cream flavor. The vanilla taste, for example, is stronger.

When it came to bread and rolls, the scientists were able to make them taste good. You would enjoy them, if you could get over the feeling that there is something wrong with green bread. Some of the most startling rolls were made by putting one layer of ordinary dough between two layers of Chlorella dough. Cookies were pleasing to those with a sweet tooth. They too were green, however.

If you fancy yourself an amateur chef, you might try your hand at cooking with algae. It's not as hard as it sounds. A number of youngsters have done it. One fifteen-year-old girl grew algae in a tank at home. Then she took it to the school laboratory, spun it in a centrifuge and heated it to obtain a powder. It was this powder that she used in her baking. She made cookies, cinnamon pinwheels, French bread and cheese swirls. You've probably heard of women entering pies and cakes in a baking contest. Well, this young girl entered her baked goods in the National Science Fair — and she won a prize for them, too.

If you are feeling ambitious, here is a cookie recipe you might try: Take two cups of cake flour, one half cup of sugar, one quarter pound of butter, one small egg and two teaspoonfuls of Chlorella. (Your science teacher can tell you where to get the algae.) You mix the ingredients together to form a dough. Then you shape the cookies with your hands, the top of a glass or a cookie cutter. Put them on a greased flat pan and pop them into the oven.

Your family will get quite a surprise when you serve these pretty green cookies for dessert.

5·

WHY EAT ALGAE?

BY NOW the thought may have struck you that green cookies are àll very well as a joke, but why bother? After all, we have plenty of lemon, orange and chocolate cookies right now. It's true that they don't contain protein, but then you can always eat meat for that.

That's true today. But it may not always be so. We are eating up the present food supplies of the world faster than they can grow again. And the population gets bigger every year. We have to build houses on land that should be kept for farming.

Look around the countryside. In much of the United States, you'll see row upon row of houses in places that used to have miles and miles of wheat or corn or grazing land for cattle. And in other parts of the world it is even worse.

Maybe you think the world is crowded now. The peo-

45

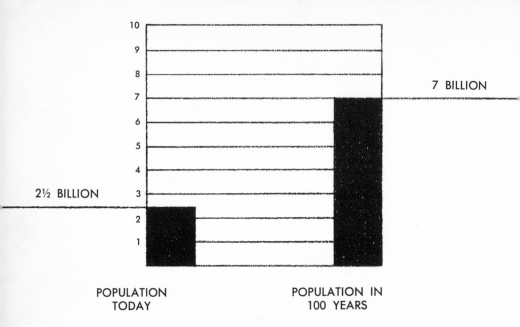

10

9

8   7 BILLION

7

6

5

4

2½ BILLION   3

2

1

POPULATION   POPULATION IN
TODAY   100 YEARS

ple in China and India certainly feel that way. And there are only a little more than two and a half billion people in the world. In a hundred years, the world's population is expected to reach a staggering total of seven billion people.

About a hundred and fifty years ago, thinking people became very frightened about the future. An English economist named Thomas Robert Malthus made studies about the growing population.

"Future generations will be poor and hungry," he said grimly, "because the population is growing too fast for the world's natural resources to keep up."

Today we feel that Malthus was too easily discouraged. He did not foresee that science could prepare for the time when the wheat that makes our bread is used up. If the time should ever come when no land at all was available

46

for farming, algae could still be grown in the laboratory from a start of a few cells!

And so algae may be the main source of food in the future, if meat, potatoes, vegetables and fruit are in short supply. But even today, they could be of benefit to mankind.

Lots of people in the world are going hungry right now. They don't eat breakfast, lunch and dinner every day, with a Coke or a candy bar in between. In parts of the world, an entire family lives on just about the amount of food you get from raiding the refrigerator. The amount may be the same, but not the quality. It doesn't include a cold hamburger, a leg of leftover chicken or a bowl of strawberries with cream. Chances are it is just rice, macaroni or a few beans. These foods are low in energy-giving protein.

The problem is that in many countries there are already too many people for the land to support. In India, for example, the population increases by close to five million a year. Even though more food is produced, bad weather can really be a matter of life or death. There are still famines so terrible that millions of people eat only one meal a day. Farmers plant their crops. And then, they dig up the roots. They know that they should wait for the crops to grow . . . but how can they? They are just too hungry. In a train robbery in India not long ago, the thieves did not bother to take money from the passengers. They found five bags of rice on board and forgot all about everything else.

Algae could help these starving people. Corn and wheat need acres of rich black farmland. Cattle must graze on acres of grass. But algae are not so demanding. All they want is light, water, carbon dioxide, nitrogen and traces of other minerals found free almost everywhere. You might think that the water would be a stumbling block for desert countries. But these plants are not fussy. The same water can be used over and over again.

Crops of algae need less space than any crop you've ever heard of. Soybeans, for example, require sixty times as much farmland.

One reason for the size of the algae harvest is that there is no waste. At least half of every other vegetable or grain is thrown away. You take an ear of corn, pull off the leaves, pick out the silky threads, and after the kernels are eaten the cob goes in the garbage pail. And the farmer has already disposed of the root and stem. Only with algae can every bit of the crop be used as human food. There is not a single root or leaf or stem to be grown, picked and thrown away. There's just one cell and all of it can be eaten.

You probably think of late summer and early fall as harvest time. And that's true for the crops we know best. But algae defy the seasons. The cells reach maturity in a few hours, so that they are ready to be harvested almost as soon as they have been planted. And as long as there is sunlight, the algae will grow. They are at the peak of their growing season all year round.

Well, what are we waiting for? If people are hungry and algae can feed them, why aren't these plants farmed on a large scale? Unfortunately, it's not so easy. Starting a whole new method of farming is expensive. And it is one of the ironies of fate that the countries that need food the most do not have enough money for the special equipment for algal farming. Many of them also lack the highly trained scientists and engineers needed to get a new system under way.

Countries like the United States could do this fairly easily. But we don't need extra food. We have plenty of corn, wheat and beef. Of the overcrowded countries with little good farming land, only Japan and Israel have the technical facilities needed to produce algae. And both have started to do so on a small scale. But to the more backward countries, eating algae is still a dream of the future.

The time is coming when hunger will be forgotten. And algae will help to bring this about. Research has been started to find ways of growing algae cheaply and to transform them into delicious foods. The search will not end until that goal has been reached.

6·

INSURANCE AGAINST HUNGER

HAVE YOU EVER imagined that you were cut off from civilization, like the early settlers surrounded by Indians? How would you manage? For a while you could live on the food you had stored in your cupboards and in the cellar. But what then?

The fear of being cut off from food supplies is not just a game or a daydream. It is a real thing. Men have been worrying about it throughout history. And they have come up with a number of ideas — none of them foolproof. During World War I, the French were besieged by the Germans. The government promptly suggested that every family buy a couple of rabbits and keep them in a hutch in the back yard. As rabbits multiply quickly, the family would always have something to eat. The catch is that a diet of rabbit does not supply all the necessary food elements. And the rabbits themselves need quite a lot to eat.

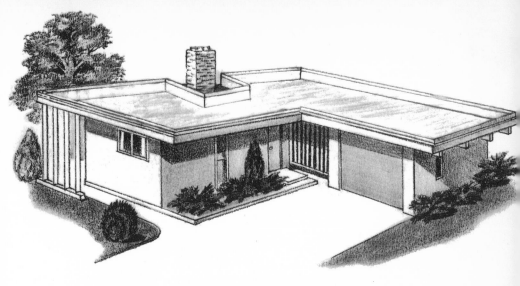

Perhaps algae will be grown
on the rooftops of houses.

No one could make these complaints about algae.
They reproduce faster than the most active rabbit. An algal
diet is rich in protein, vitamins, starches and minerals. As
for its own food, no plant or animal is less demanding than
are algae.

By planning ahead, the settlers in the blockade or the
inhabitants of a beleaguered city could guarantee themselves a never-ending source of food. They could build
themselves houses with algae tanks on the roof. They could
then be barricaded for years without ever running out of
food.

This sounds like one of those farfetched ideas you read
about in comic books. But it is actually quite sound. Scientists have been considering such a scheme seriously, preparing for a time when food may become really scarce. Dr.
Hans Gaffron of the University of Chicago has already
drawn up blueprints for a house where algae can be grown
on the rooftop.

It is an average-sized ranch house, with a flat roof extending beyond the side walls. The roof itself measures 62 by 100 feet. This size was not just chosen by chance. It is based on the most careful figuring. A typical family of five or six people eat a little less than four and a half pounds of protein a day. This is just about the amount that could be harvested from the 62-by-100-foot roof.

The way it works is that about two inches of water with algae in it is pumped over the roof. The carbon dioxide to nourish the plants is gotten by burning garbage, and the needed chemicals come from human wastes. These are sterilized before being added to the water. You can see that the family living in this house doesn't need to depend on any outsiders.

How about light for photosynthesis? Sunlight is free for everyone and the algae on the roof are right in the path of the brilliant rays. For this reason, algae houses are planned for moderate climates only. You may see them in southern California or parts of Texas; they will never be a part of a housing development in Alaska or Siberia. The little plants stop growing during a long, dark winter.

The algal roof keeps the family both well-fed and comfortable. The layer of water absorbs the heat of the sun and cools the house during the summer. The only danger is that the suspension (algae plus water and chemicals) can become too hot for even the high-temperature algae. And so a method has been worked out, hooking up the suspension to a chemical cooling system. In the winter, this system can go into reverse and heat the house. During the summer the chemicals in the cooling system take in the heat from the suspension and store it. As soon as the temperature drops below a certain point, the heat is released, and warms both the algae and the house. This method of cooling and heating is called a solar heating system, and has already been used successfully in model homes around Boston.

Building a house like this would cost a lot, but not as much as you might think. The price at first will be about five times as high as for an ordinary house.

Algal rooftop homes are not likely to dot the country-side during your lifetime. But your great-great-grandchildren may take them as a matter of course.

In the meantime, a good deal of thought is being given to producing algae in large enough quantities to provide a little of this wholesome and nourishing food for everyone.

But getting algae into production is surprisingly difficult. It is all very well to say that you see the one-celled algae every day as the scum on the top of stagnant ponds or the green film on rocks and trees. But you can hardly skim off a little and eat it. If algae are to become part of a nation's food supply, they have to be farmed and harvested.

As algae farming is water farming; no soil at all is needed. The "farm" can be placed on a huge flat rooftop. This is simply a big-scale version of the individual rooftop house. Of course, the farmers can't depend upon their own wastes to nourish the microscopic plants. They must find some other source. In one test farm, sea water was used, as it has most of the needed chemicals in it.

When enough algae have grown, they are simply scooped off the top. Then they are dried. So far, the farmers haven't tried eating algae themselves. But the local cattle have been delighted to get some in their feed.

Like the rooftop house, this type of farm is most suited to warm sunny climates, as in southern California. In cool climates, the need for artificial lighting and heat add considerably to the cost.

As a matter of fact, algae can be produced in any modern city for almost nothing. The method doesn't sound pretty but it works. Algae can be grown in sewage. Every American city has a pond or plant where wastes are gathered and disposed of. And sewage can give algae every essential chemical. As we have seen, this is one of the advantages of using algae in the photosynthetic gas exchanger for spaceships.

Two scientists, Drs. H. B. Gotaas and W. J. Oswald of the University of California, have grown algae in sewage disposal ponds. You might think that these microscopic plants would be dirty and dangerous to use as food. But after they are dried under intense heat, the sewage pond algae are completely free of germs.

Dr. Gotaas even insists that the pond does not smell bad. The algae conquer the odors of decay and sewage, and the resulting smell is like that of grass or hay.

The scientists have figured out that the sewage from a city of 100,000 people could produce ten tons of dry algae a day. In addition, ten million gallons of water, which could be used for irrigation of dry lands, are gotten as a by-product.

The sewage method of growing algae appeals to city officials because it is a way of making money, instead of spending. It now costs about $500 a day to take care of a typical city's sewage. The algae could be sold for at least six cents a pound, bringing in about $1,200 a day. As it would cost quite a lot to build a plant, this is not all profit. But the city still ends up ahead.

Some sewage is sold for use as fertilizer, but a number of city officials report that the United States throws away sewage that could produce 10,000 tons of dried algae a

Tokugawa Institute for
Biological Research

Culture ponds of algae in Japan

day. That's more protein than is grown on a million acres of land in a whole year.

Of course, you would not eat sewage-pond algae, even if you knew they were good for you. You would be disgusted at the very idea. And so algae coming from those lowly origins would probably be used to feed animals.

You may be thinking that in countries where people are starving, they would not be so fussy. That is quite true. Unfortunately, most of these countries could not use this method for the simple reason that they have no sewage disposal systems.

Japan is one of the few highly developed countries to have the problem of a big population and a small amount of land on which to grow food. And so it is not surprising that a great deal of work has been done there to develop good ways of growing algae. The Japanese were

55

the first to get an algal farm going. At the moment, it is a small one. But there are big plans for the next few years.

The Japanese system takes the rooftop farm and brings it down to earth. The result would surprise any American farmer. The farm consists mainly of open shallow ponds. Chlorella, carbon dioxide and chemicals are dumped into the ponds. Underwater pipes keep the mixture moving. When enough algae have grown, some of the liquid is pumped out of the pond and sent to a control house. There the algal cells are separated from the water and are dried. In the last stage, the Chlorella is ground in a mill to form a powder. This is then added to ice cream, bread, macaroni, cake, milk powder and other foods.

The cost of the algae is high, but much of the powder is mixed with other, cheaper foods. And as the Japanese need extra protein badly, they foresee a great future for algal farming in their country.

A Japanese scientist, Dr. Hiroshi Nakamura of the Japan Microalgae Research Institute, has come up with yet another suggestion for algal farming that is remarkably simple and efficient. His idea is to make an outdoor, over-sized aquarium.

Carp, tropical fish, goldfish, eels and other fresh-water fish are placed in a pond with Chlorella in it. The fish give carbon dioxide and minerals to the algae. And that's not all they do. By swimming around, they stir the tiny plants, encouraging them to grow. The fish are a natural substitute for the pumps needed in other systems.

When enough algae have grown, they are drawn out of the pond by a suction pump. The mouth of the pump has to be covered with wire netting, so that the fish do not accompany the algae out of the pond.

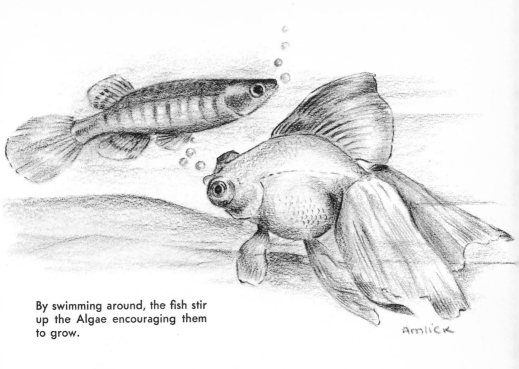

By swimming around, the fish stir up the Algae encouraging them to grow.

Amlick

A pond that is about 650 feet in diameter could produce over thirteen pounds of dried algae a day. And when you got tired of algae stew, you could eat the fish.

Dr. Nakamura suggests that a similar system could be used on board spaceships. The fish would be imprisoned in a glass tank, instead of swimming freely in a pond. Extra light for photosynthesis could be gotten by connecting a small fluorescent light bulb to the tail of each fish. Some of the fish would be added to the crew's dinner menu, to provide a welcome change.

"In traveling through space, which is a world of dead silence," adds the Japanese scientist, "the crew will get great pleasure from feasting their eyes on the swimming fish."

7.

ON THE ASSEMBLY LINE

EVER SINCE Henry Ford first found a way of building cars on the assembly line, the United States has been
mass-production-happy. As soon as it became obvious that
algae could be made into a highly nutritious food, engineers
went to work. Clearly, they thought, it should be no harder
to make algae than to make Fords.

"We started by considering algae as an industrial
product, rather than a farm crop," explains an engineer.
"As algae don't ask for land, they could be grown in a huge
manufacturing plant.

"We didn't start right out by building such a factory,"
he added. "What we did was to set up a pilot plant."

That is an experimental factory, done on a very small
scale. The reason for using a model or test plant is that any
new production method is risky. The designs may look
good on the drawing boards; the theory may seem sound

Arthur D. Little, Inc.

Algae pilot plant

when explained by the engineers. But somehow the finished factory is a failure. The machines don't do the job they were supposed to. As it costs millions of dollars to build a big industrial plant, no one is willing to take such a gamble. And so a miniature version is built instead. If it can turn out one car or one pound of algae, it works — and a bigger one could work, too. It is also possible to multiply the cost of the raw materials, equipment and labor by ten, one thousand or one million and come up with a pretty accurate figure for the cost of a really good-sized factory.

A few years ago, Arthur D. Little, Inc., of Cambridge, Massachusetts, set up an algal pilot plant. The basic principle of the plant was the same as that of the rooftop farms described in the last chapter. But the planning was for

The chlorella was moved to huge containers on the roof

real mass production, with heavy processing equipment on the lower floors of one huge building.

The whole operation started with a little flask of Chlorella grown in the laboratory. These algae were then transferred to ten upright columns made of Pyrex glass. They were set up out of doors facing south, so as to get the advantage of the sunshine. Then came the most important part: the Chlorella was moved to huge containers or tubes on the roof of the factory building.

These containers were not made of glass or steel or any other metal that you might expect to find. They were made of the same flimsy plastic that is used to make bags for packaged carrots and oranges in the supermarket and to protect clothes when they have been dry-cleaned. It is called polyethylene.

As far as the algae are concerned, polyethylene has the tremendous advantage of being transparent. The sunlight can come right through to the tiny plants. From the viewpoint of the businessmen financing the factory, this plastic has the advantage of being cheap.

The tubing made for the Arthur D. Little company was an incredibly fragile 0.004 of an inch thick and was eight feet in circumference. It was bent into the shape of a U. After it was set up on the roof, 1,200 gallons of water, carbon dioxide, chemical nutrients and Chlorella were poured into it. This algal suspension filled the tubing to a height of about two and a half inches.

In the tubing, the Chlorella was to lead the same sort of life it would have in a natural outdoor pond. But the scientists wanted to improve on nature.

"Our algae should grow even better than in an outdoor pond," they said.

Two of the greatest men in algae research, Drs. H. A. Spoehr and Howard Milner of the Carnegie Institute, California, found studies of prehistoric days revealing that algae had been more plentiful then. Why? There was, of course, no one for them to ask. They had to find the reason by trial and error. And at last they discovered that carbon dioxide was the key. In prehistoric times, the atmosphere contained 5 per cent of this gas, while today air has only 0.03 of it. And so the proportion of carbon dioxide that was common in days before man walked the earth was fed into the supermodern polyethylene tubing in the pilot plant.

Nitrogen, magnesium, phosphorus, potassium and other chemicals were also added.

The best lighting system in the world — the sun — was used to trigger photosynthesis. That was the whole idea of placing the tubing on the roof.

"We decided to kill two birds with one stone," reports

a research man, "by finding a way of giving algae alternate periods of light and darkness and keeping them moving as well. Both these conditions encourage them to grow. And so we designed a pump that could stir up the suspension in such a way that algae would be brought to the top of the tubing into the sunshine and then plunged back into the darkness at the bottom. The cells in the top layer in this way change from minute to minute."

Even so, it gets pretty hot on the roof, and the pump cannot keep the Chlorella out of the way of the heat. A cooling device had to be added.

Nature provides hazards besides heat. Some of these took the engineers by surprise, as most industrial equipment does not face the great outdoors. One day, for example, there was a severe storm, with gusts of wind reaching ninety miles an hour. The wind tore gravel off neighboring houses and threw it against the tubing. Holes were punctured in the thin plastic, and much of the Chlorella was lost.

"There is really no way to guard against this sort of thing," says an engineer. "We just had to mark it up to loss, repair the tubing and get production going again."

After the Chlorella had been given time to multiply, some of the suspension was taken out of the tubing and moved downstairs to a huge centrifuge. This spinning machine separated the solid algae from the water. The liquid was sent back upstairs and thrown back into the tubing. This would be a tremendous advantage in algae production in desert countries where water is more valuable than gold. What remains after the water is removed is a heavy green paste.

"What is that unpleasant smell?" asked a scientist

entering the room where the Chlorella paste was lying.

There was only one thing to blame: the Chlorella itself. It could not endure even a few hours at room temperature. And so the paste had to be either frozen or dried immediately.

"Drying is considered the most practical," says an engineer, "as algae must be in a dry form before being processed into food."

Algae were grown and harvested in this way for several months. At the end of that time it was clear that mass production was possible. The engineers figured out that a full-sized plant occupying one hundred acres could make 12,500 pounds of dry algae per day.

But will such a plant ever be built? At the moment, it does not look that way. What is the catch? Expense. The scientists and engineers found themselves with a good product that would simply cost too much for people to buy. The price tag on algae would be at least 25 cents a pound. This figure may not sound high to you when you think of what steak or chops cost at the supermarket. But who will eat algae when steak is available?

Algologists could only hope that the Little engineers had been too extravagant in their production techniques. A few years after the Little experiment, another firm, Chas. Pfizer & Co. of Brooklyn, New York, set up its own pilot plant to see if costs could not be lowered. They were not so lucky. Their findings showed that the algae would have to sell for 50 cents a pound, and possibly as much as a dollar.

Some Chlorella could be processed and added to other foods, as is being done in Japan. But in the United States where food is plentiful, much of the algae is earmarked for animal feed. And most of the farm products commonly used in feed today are priced at from six to ten cents a pound.

This doesn't mean that algae will never come into mass production here. Scientists have not given up. They are determined to find ways of making algae cheaply. Improvements in design of equipment and the discovery of new strains of algae could bring prices of these plants down to the economy level.

The new high-temperature strain of Chlorella, for example, was discovered in Texas too late to be used in either of these pilot plant projects. It might do away with the expensive cooling equipment. In addition, as this strain multiplies so fast, the amount of algae produced per day would be much higher. And there may be even more efficient algae lying unknown in the deserts of Arizona or beneath the ice in Alaska.

"Don't take the cost figures too seriously," advises a leading figure in the food industry. "In the last few years, many food products that once seemed absurdly expensive to make have become a part of our daily diets."

Just think of coffee. Green coffee beans have to be brought from countries thousands of miles away, roasted in huge plants, ground and packed in cans. A generation ago, people would have been staggered by the cost of the equipment needed to squeeze oranges, make a concentrate of the juice and freeze it. Today frozen orange juice and coffee are taken for granted in almost every home in the United States.

Men have figured out ways of transforming raw cocoa beans into candy bars, and putting tomatoes into ketchup bottles. It is not too much to expect that they will be able to work the same magic with algae.

8

HOW ABOUT STRAINING THE SEA?

CAN YOU IMAGINE running the sea through a huge strainer? What would you get? Gigantic whales and sharks, porpoises, tuna, herring, maybe some seaweed. And then, stuck to the very bottom of the strainer, there would be . . . something. You woudn't be quite sure what it was — plants, animals, scum.

If you emptied your sieve onto a table and looked with a strong magnifying glass at the mess that poured out, you would discover that it was made up of millions and millions of tiny algae, infinitesimal shrimp, fish eggs, crabs that would fit on the point of a needle, miniature fish and a wealth of other unbelievably small living things. One inch of your table would hold between three thousand and six thousand of these plants and animals.

They have a strange name, "plankton." This was originally a Greek word meaning "wandering." And that is

exactly what these primitive plants and creatures do. Even the animals in the group do not swim. They are carried hither and thither at the whim of the ocean currents.

Plankton were first discovered more than a hundred years ago by a German scientist named Johannes Mueller. He made a net of finely meshed muslin and towed it alongside his boat. Big fish were able to avoid him. But not the microscopic forms of life. Years later, it was discovered that most of the phytoplankton, as the plant members of the family are called, are algae. The miniscule fishlike animals were given the name of zooplankton.

Both existed for millions of years before Mr. Mueller noticed them. Scientists trying to peer back through the ages to discover facts about the earth when it was young use plankton as a living reference book. They gather sediment from the bottom of the ocean and carefully study the plankton in each layer of mud. A short time ago with this method, they learned that the ice-locked Arctic Basin had not always been cold. Russian scientists raised a layer of gray sandy mud from the ocean floor and found only a few algae and animals in it. They had expected this beneath the harsh sub-zero waters. But then they came to a layer of brown mud, containing the remains of a type of plankton which can live only in warm climates. The history of those prehistoric days is written in the plankton.

As you might expect from their continued existence, plankton only seem to be helpless. They are actually extremely well equipped in the struggle for survival. The zooplankton use some of the algae as food. And these in turn get nourishment from the chemicals which are formed from dead animal plankton. It's almost a perfect circle.

Luckily the plankton reproduce in such great quanti-

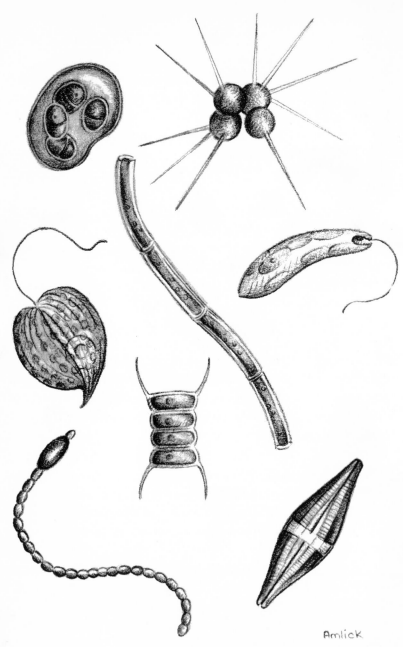

**Phytoplankton or plant plankton
greatly enlarged**

Amlick

ties that they are not all eaten up by members of their own family. These infinitesimal algae and fish are among the most important living things in the entire world. Fish, sea birds and sea animals owe their very lives to the plankton.

An old Chinese proverb says: "Big fish eat little fish, little fish eat shrimp, shrimp eat mud."

This seemingly simple saying contains a real scientific truth. That mud on the bottom of the ocean contains plankton.

When you were little, you probably played with a toy that has amused generations of children. At first you thought you had been given just one big box. But when you opened it, you found a smaller one inside. Within that there was another still smaller, and so on.

A few years ago, a scientist performed that same trick with a little fish. He cut open its stomach and found it filled with tiny herring. Taking out the herrring, he slit their stomachs and discovered still smaller fishes within. He cut open the stomachs of these minute fishes and found that they were filled with algae. One biologist was able to spot 150 different species of algae in the digestive tract of a single fish.

And you can be certain that this fish was not suffering from any nutritional deficiencies. Laboratory tests show that plankton are nearly 60 per cent protein. This is even higher than the claims made for everybody's favorite, Chlorella. The scientists also reported large amounts of vitamins.

There is some reason to believe that the plankton act both as food and medicine for marine life. One day a number of zoologists made a thorough examination of penguins. In the stomachs of these black and white birds, they were surprised to find some organisms that worked like antibiotics, killing germs and bacteria. The men went on to analyze the stomach contents more carefully. And sure enough, their trail eventually led them to tiny green algae.

These plants perform their useful work in cold seas and warm. Plankton can be found all over the globe — wherever there is water. That, of course, is practically everywhere. Nearly three-quarters of the earth's surface is covered by water. You might consider the seas and oceans as a nourishing soup. The nourishment comes from the plankton. Shipwrecked sailors have sometimes died of hunger, not knowing that they were surrounded by food.

We usually think that the days of shipwrecked mariners are far behind us. But even today, many people are cast adrift on the vast oceans. Ships still sink and airplanes are sometimes forced down over water. The passengers must take to lifeboats or rafts. If you should ever be in that spot, remember plankton.

Anyone lost at sea naturally thinks of improvising some sort of crude fishing line. But in many parts of the ocean, there are few edible fish. And those may refuse to snap at a line without tempting bait. So you would be wise to make a net out of your shirt or sweater and tow it behind your boat or raft. Every few hours, you would pull in the net, scrape off the plankton catch and eat it. This has been done by sailors adrift on the oceans — sailors who survived.

Not everyone who takes to sea on a raft is shipwrecked. Some people do it for adventure or for scientific expeditions. A few years ago a Norwegian scientist named Thor Heyerdahl came up with an interesting theory. He believed that hundreds and hundreds of years ago, the Indians of Peru sailed across the Pacific on handmade rafts and settled on the South Sea Islands. Everybody laughed at him. It is impossible to cross the Pacific on a raft, they told him. To prove his point, Heyerdahl decided that he would make that trip himself, taking five companions with him.

They were able to carry some food, but not enough for the whole voyage. They had to count on catching fish and gathering plankton. They armed themselves with a special silk net so fine that there were three thousand meshes in every square inch. The miniscule algae and animals could not slip through to escape. Heyerdahl and his men towed this net behind the raft, pulling it in every few hours to see what they had caught. In many parts of the Pacific, they were able to gather several pounds in a short time. At some places they drew in red plankton, in others brown or brownish-gray or green plankton. At night, they found that certain of the plankton sparkled with a magical phosphorescence.

A part of the catch was eaten raw; the rest was cooked in water to make a plankton chowder. The men soon learned to take out tiny jellyfish, as these had a bitter taste. What was left tasted something like lobster, crab or shrimp paste. Once in a while they got plankton that tasted like oysters, or like that rare delicacy, caviar.

You don't need to be desperate for food or be traveling across the Pacific on a raft to enjoy eating shellfish. That is one of the reasons why scientists believe that plankton could have a big future as a human food. The flavor of the shrimplike zooplankton wins out over the dried lima bean taste of the algae. Although Chlorella with artificial flavoring added gets the most attention as a possible food of the future, plankton will probably serve as a healthful side dish.

But you can't just go around munching on any plankton that come your way. Some species are poisonous. If you live in Florida, California or Texas, you have probably seen poisonous plankton without knowing it. The famous "red tides" which color the water at certain times of the year are caused by red, poisonous plankton. These tides are not limited to the United States; they are also found on the coasts of Peru, Japan, India, Australia and parts of Africa and Europe.

When the "red tides" come in, fishermen abandon their fishing poles, clam pots and nets. They know that no one could eat anything they caught. The fish would be dead anyway, victims of the poison. But the shellfish remain perfectly well. They thrive on plankton, good or bad. Unfortunately, if any human being or animal eats a shellfish that has been gorging itself on poisonous plankton, he will become ill. The poison in a clam has been found to be ten times as deadly to mice as is strychnine.

Even some of the blue-green algae are poisonous. Horses have died after eating plants of this type on some of the coral beaches on the coast of India. In the United States, cases of skin infections and hay fever have been reported by people who touched some blue-green algae on the beaches of fresh-water lakes.

But those planning to use plankton as food point out that it is perfectly easy to stick to the wholesome types.

"Even primitive populations learned to avoid the poisonous plankton," states Dr. Luigi Provasoli, noted algologist of the Haskins Laboratories, New York. "It is a part of the folklore in every area where 'red tides' exist that clams or mussels should not be eaten at certain seasons. And dead fish are left strictly alone by fishermen."

What primitive men can do, we can do, too. And efforts are being made in the laboratory to discover just what makes certain plankton poisonous. Once this is known, it may be possible to prevent the development of the poison, or to control its spread.

Plankton does so much good that it seems unfair to condemn the whole family because of the bad behavior of a few of its members. The whole fish population of the ocean depends either directly or indirectly on these microscopic plants and animals. Today farsighted men are considering ways of improving the balance of nature. Parts of the ocean contain very few fish. One reason is that the fish there do not have enough to eat. Marine biologists believe that if fish were brought to places where plankton are plentiful, they would thrive on the rich diet. They would grow bigger and reproduce in large numbers. The result would be an increase in the world's food supply.

What parts of the sea are most crowded with algae and miniature animals? New types of ocean maps are being made. "X" marks the spot where the plankton congregate. There are already maps of the Atlantic Ocean showing the distribution of the seventeen most important species. The Scottish Oceanographic Laboratory has made a similar chart of the North Sea. Government officials are most interested today in the map being made of the Indian Ocean all the way from Indonesia to South Africa. This ocean touches many countries with large populations and small supplies of food. People there would welcome an extra helping of fish. It would lend variety to the diet many of them eat — rice today, rice tomorrow, rice the day after.

"Starving men do not insist on filet of flounder — or any recognizable fish, for that matter," says a nutrition expert. "They would be happy to eat the plankton. The sad thing is that even though the maps show us where the algae and minute animals are, nothing shows us how to collect them."

In most parts of the world, the sea would literally have to be run through a sieve. A ton of sea water has to be filtered in order to get .03 of an ounce of plankton. At this rate, it would take days to get enough for a single plank-tonburger.

There are some places, however, where plankton are so plentiful that they can be seen by the naked eye. It is possible to collect these plants and animals more easily there. In Venezuela, Dr. Jorgen Jorgensen reported that all he needed to do to get plankton was to scoop up water from Maracaibo Lake and filter it through a couple of old felt hats.

In Thailand, about five thousand tons are harvested from the sea every year. Most of it is eaten in the form of a paste, something like anchovy paste. Some is mixed with other foods.

During World War II, Great Britain was so short of food that meat, fats and many other staples were rationed. At that time, the idea of eating plankton became appealing. A British scientist, A. C. Hardy, figured that with suitable nets, two men on the coast of Scotland could gather 588 pounds of plankton a day. This would be enough to feed 357 people. This project never really got off the ground. It would have been harder than it sounds anyway. The very fine nets that must be used clog easily.

Machines are being designed to do the job more efficiently. One has been invented that could get the plankton out of Lake Ontario at the point where it runs into the

Saint Lawrence River. Hundreds of thousands of gallons of water would be handled. At present, this process is so expensive that businessmen are turning thumbs down on it. But if foods grow scarce, it may seem worth doing.

One firm in the United States is already producing plankton. That is the American Food and Drug Manufacturing Corporation in Clayton, Ohio. But so far, it only grows enough to be used in research both in America and in foreign countries. The cost is $10 a pound. In the future, this company plans to increase production and sell plankton for animal feed and human food as well. At that point, executives think they'll be able to bring prices down to 37 cents a pound.

But if plankton are to join planked steak in your regular diet, the number of them must be increased to the point where they are easy to collect anywhere in the world. Men must find ways of "fertilizing the sea." This phrase means just what you think it does. Phosphates, nitrates and other chemicals that encourage plankton to grow must be thrown into the ocean.

This idea frightens the experts just as much as it would alarm you, if you were asked to give it a try. How would you go about adding fertilizers to the sea? Would you go down to the beach and toss them in by the barrelful? Wouldn't they be lost in millions and millions of gallons of water?

Unfortunately, that is just about the way it works. So far there has been some success at fertilizing inlets, bays, lakes or ponds. In these, much of the fertilizer stays put, instead of being swept out to the open sea. The catch here is that these inland and coastal waters do not really need additional fertilizers. The rich soil washing into them has already done the job. And adding anything to the gigantic ocean is a project so vast that it simply staggers the mind. But don't write it off. Many scientists think that it could be done. If the world ever faces a real food shortage, every way of adding to the food supply will be tried.

Man's imagination has always been challenged by the dream of the day when the sea will be made to give up its treasures. Some people think of sunken ships and buried caskets of coins and jewels lying below our reach. If you are interested in science, you may be fascinated by the thought of the vast amount of gold that is in the ocean water itself. Surely some inexpensive easy way could be found to separate it from the vast seas.

But today we are beginning to realize that the oceans contain treasures less romantic than jewels and gold . . . but much more valuable to the starving of the world. When the sea is forced to give up its plankton treasure, men will be saved from hunger.

Other foods may be used up in the next two or three hundred years. All land may be needed to house the huge populations of the future. But century after century, the tides will rise and fall, bringing with them food for mankind.

9.

INSIDE ALGAE

ONE DAY in the distant future, your great-great-grandchildren will get up from their breakfast of algal krispies and freshly baked green rolls and complain that the house is cold.

"I guess I'd better go down to the basement and turn up the algal oil burner," their father will say.

In the world of tomorrow described by the economists, not only food supplies, but also coal and oil may be used up. We burn larger amounts of fuel every year. As the population grows, more houses are built, each with a heating system. Factories need electric power to make appliances, cars and clothes for these additional people. What will happen when the last drop of oil and chunk of coal has been dropped into the burners? What will replace them?

Once again the most primitive of the earth's plants will come to the rescue. Algae may be both the food and the fuel of the future.

The University of California scientists who have been busy growing algae in sewage disposal plants have found that a valuable by-product is made at the bottom of the pond. Dead algae cells drift down into the muck where they are attacked by bacteria. A gas is formed when decayed matter and bacteria meet. This gas is called methane, and can be used as fuel.

"This natural method of making methane can be copied in a big way in a manufacturing plant," chemists report. "The algae are grown in the laboratory of the factory. In time, some of the cells die. Then we bring in the bacteria. They invade the decaying plant tissue and form gases."

These gases can be treated to make two liquid fuels which you see and use all the time — kerosene and gasoline.

"We figure that between six and nine tons of liquid fuel can be gotten from thirty-five tons of algae," add the chemists.

As is true of all revolutionary ideas, the process is still very expensive.

"What if it is?" asks one scientist. "We could work out a method to get food from some of the algae and fuel from the rest. This would make it a good deal all around."

Algae can also be made into a solid fuel on the order of coal or charcoal. Algal coal is very much like medium-grade bituminous coal, the kind that is used all the time today. It does not give off quite as much heat, however. And it is much harder to make solid algal fuel than to use it as the basis for a gas or liquid.

"It's getting dark. I'll turn on the algal electric light," those great-great-grandchildren of yours may say one day in another century.

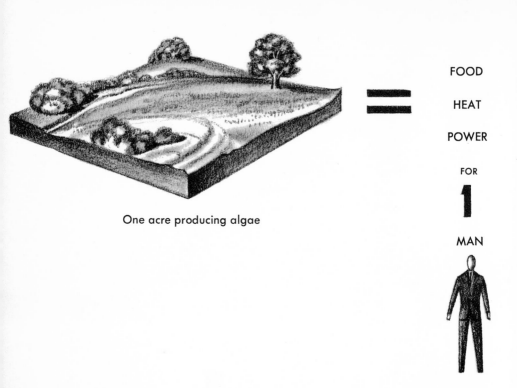

One acre producing algae

= FOOD HEAT POWER FOR 1 MAN

This idea may seem strange to you at first, but when you think it over, it makes good sense. Nowadays electric power is usually gotten from generators driven by burning coal or oil. The same results could be gotten by burning algae. When the plants grow, the sun's energy is stored within their cells. This energy is released when the algae are burned, and can be used as the basis for electric power. The scientific name for the machine that is needed for this system is an "algal energy converter." These words may some day be familiar to every school child.

If oil, coal and farm products really were used up and the world had to depend upon algae for fuel and food, how much would be needed? Would you care to make a guess? A number of men have gazed into their scientific crystal balls and have come up with this figure: one acre of land (or a rooftop farm, if there were no free land) would produce enough algae to provide food, heat and electricity for *one* person. With this information, you may be able to work out how much 100 people, or 1,000, or even 1,000,000 would need. In 100 years the population is expected to reach seven billion. If all these people were to depend on algae, eleven million square miles of the earth would have to be given over to these plants. This figure sounds tremendous. But it is actually less than one-fifth of the land surface of the earth. If that small area could give your descendants all the food and fuel they needed, they would have no cause to worry.

Algal fuel and food are only a part of what the future holds. Modern scientists are like the old prospectors for gold. Instead of panning shimmering rock in search of the valuable metal, they are analyzing the algae cells. And they are finding some rare chemical elements. There are claims being staked out for germanium, a valuable and very scarce element. Germanium is particularly useful in making transistors and other electric equipment. It can't be damaged by contact with the air, water or even most of the powerful acids. You can see how much could be done with such a substance.

Unfortunately, there is very little of it in the world — none lying around loose. The ore, germanite, holds only 6 per cent of germanium. Most of the element must be taken from ores of zinc, lead and copper, a little at a time. A bit more is gotten from the ashes of certain coals. Now we learn that germanium lies within the algae cells. The prob-

81

lem is to get it out. If a good process could be found, it would make all the work that has been done on algae worth while indeed.

But germanium is just one of the wonderful substances to be gotten from "mining" these tiny plants. The most obvious is chlorophyll, which can be used to kill bad smells. A number of drug manufacturers, therefore, add it to toothpaste, mouthwash and other products.

Algae are not the only plants to contain chlorophyll. Every green plant has some. It wouldn't be green if it hadn't. This substance not only gives plants their color, it also makes it possible for them to grow. The whole process of photosynthesis could not go on without chlorophyll. Photosynthesis, you may recall, is the process by which plants take in carbon dioxide, water and fertilizers and turn them into sugars and starches, releasing oxygen at the same time. No plant has quite as much chlorophyll as do algae. They have between twenty and thirty times as much as does alfalfa, which is now the main source.

In addition to chlorophyll, plants contain coloring matter that can be used to make paints and dyes. The best known of these is called carotene, and has a brilliant yellow color. You probably expected this, because the name sounds so much like the word "carrot." Chlorella and many of the other green algae are just chock-full of carotene.

At present, most paint manufacturers feel that carotene is too expensive to be used as a source of color. They are more interested in the fats contained in the algal cells. More than one-fifth of the Chlorella cell is made up of fats. And the percentage could be made even higher by some scientific abracadabra. When these tiny plants are starved by depriving them of nitrogen, the amount of protein decreases and the fat increases. Hungry Chlorella, unlike people or animals, gets fatter and fatter. As much as 86 per cent of the starved Chlorella cell may be made up of fats. These can be treated to become a special kind of oil, known as drying oil. This is added to paint to make it dry quickly. It is not really necessary to create particularly fat algae; just plain Chlorella can be used to make drying oils. As all work with algae is expensive, the idea is to get some drying oils as an extra dividend when growing the plants for food or fuel. And so the family of the future may paint its algal rooftop house with algal paint.

Sometimes it seems that algae have something to offer everyone. There are so many different ways in which these tiny plants can be used. The paint industry is interested in drying oils and the bright yellow color of carotene. Food and drug manufacturers want carotene, too, for another reason. This substance can not only be used as a coloring matter, but also as a source of vitamin A. This is an example of the miracles performed in the plant kingdom.

Vitamin A is just one of the many vitamins stored in the algae cells.

"We have corrected the old saying: 'An apple a day keeps the doctor away,' " algologists declare. "The way we say it is: 'A little algae a day keeps the doctor away.' "

A quarter of a pound of dried Chlorella a day would provide you with every single vitamin you need, except C. And that vitamin exists in raw algae; it just gets lost in the drying. When artificially flavored algae appear on the supermarket shelf, people will be able to follow the advice of the algologists. But today, almost every American would rather eat a juicy red apple than a plateful of green Chlorella. Scientists, therefore, must bow to public opinion and find some way of taking the vitamins out of the algae. These could then be added to other foods or made into vitamin pills.

So far getting vitamins out of algae remains an impractical dream. Every method tried has been too expensive and has yielded only small amounts of vitamins. But in medical research, a breakthrough can come any day.

Fish, sea animals and sea birds are being kept in good shape with antibiotics. They don't take a spoonful of Terramycin every five hours or get a shot of penicillin. They eat algae, which do the same sort of job. Scientists get a gleam in their eyes whenever they hear about this. They believe that at some time these plants could be a major source of antibiotics for human use.

When medical researchers today peer into their culture flasks of algae, they are really most interested in ways of getting hormones out of these one-celled plants. Hormones are chemicals which in human beings and animals are produced by the glands. If you are interested in recent medical discoveries, you have surely heard of cortisone. This is a wonder drug, made out of compounds called steroids. It is used in the treatment of rheumatoid arthritis and many other serious ailments. In 1948, when cortisone was tested for the first time, patients who had been bedridden for years got up and walked.

Unluckily, this drug is both expensive and scarce. It was first discovered in 1936. By 1941, doctors were ready to test it, but they simply could not get enough of it. It took seven long years for them to receive the tiny amount they needed for tests. And no one could say that the doctors were too demanding. They started the tests at a time when the entire world supply amounted to only one-eighteenth of an ounce!

Natural cortisone is made from cattle bile, the fluid produced in an animal's liver. And it takes about *forty* head of cattle to provide the bile to make enough cortisone to treat *one* arthritic patient for one day. The process of making the drug is so complicated that it requires thirty-seven separate steps.

"We have developed a number of methods of making artificial cortisone in the laboratory," say medical researchers. "At least they cut out the need for gathering bile from huge herds of cattle. But making cortisone is still terribly difficult and fabulously expensive. We keep telling ourselves that there must be an easier and cheaper way. We are looking for a new source of the steroids needed to make cortisone."

These compounds are found within the cells of some members of the green algae group, called *scenedesmus obliquus*. Already, in experiments, the steroids have been taken out of the algae cells. This research has only gotten started, but doctors are hopeful that algae might serve as the basis of this almost miraculous drug.

Breaking down the algae cell is keeping all types of scientists busy. Nutrition experts quite naturally are excited by the fact that the cells are more than half protein. Why not take the protein out of the algae and use it to improve foods? they ask. This might be even more efficient than cooking with algae. The protein could be added to bread, making it as good for you as a hearty piece of meat. Laboratory rats have already been served a bit of bread of this type along with their meals and quickly got bigger and stronger. And for once, the cost factor does not rear its ugly head. The protein threonine can be made more cheaply from algae than from any other source.

You probably hear a lot about the high cost of steak

and roasts. Everybody wishes that the economical cuts of meat were as tender as a sirloin or rib roast beef. For several years, meat tenderizers have been on the market. These are chemicals that work on tough muscle and tissue and make them soft and tender. Now researchers have found that algae contain glutamic acid, a chemical which can be used to make meat tenderizers. The end product will not be completely new, of course. But there is always the hope that algal meat tenderizers will work better or be cheaper.

We may be coming into an age when foods will be improved by algae. Antibiotics and hormones may be made from them. Manufacturers may take coloring matter and drying oils, chlorophyll and rare elements from these tiny green plants. These are only a few of the roles that algae may some day play in nutrition, medicine and industry. All over the world, men are waiting for the reports to come out of the laboratories where scientists are bending over culture flasks of algae.

10·

NATURE'S LITTLE HELPER

IN MANY PARTS of the world, people shudder when the word "drought" is spoken. To them it doesn't just mean that there has been no rain for a long time. It means famine . . . children going hungry, animals dying. Even in the United States, a long period of drought still brings tragedy to farmers, to ranchers who must watch their herds of cattle die for want of good green grass to eat.

Science has found many ways of fighting drought. Water can be brought by pipes over great distances and pumped over dry lands. Canals and ditches can be dug to carry it from rivers or reservoirs. But in many countries the people do not have the technical knowledge or the equipment needed for large-scale irrigation. Their only defenses against drought and its accompanying famine are the ones that nature offers them. Luckily, every country — rich or poor — has algae. These plants are nature's gift to drought-stricken areas.

If you have ever traveled over the cracked dry land of a region suffering from a drought, you may have noticed a greenish crust over the ground. This is an algal crust. It looks unappealing, but it serves a purpose. During periods of extreme dryness, soil turns to dust and can be blown away. The algae help to hold the land, and protect it against erosion.

Algae can stand up to drought much better than any of the higher plants. When the blazing, merciless sun beats down day after day and week after week, the grass dies, the wheat, corn and barley crops dry up and wither. Only the algae remain alive. Even they stop growing . . . but they are ready to grow again on a second's notice. At the first hint of dampness in the air, the algae start reproducing again. They do not even wait for the rain to fall. These microscopic plants can absorb the wetness in the air long before it strikes the earth. As they multiply, they enrich the soil. They make it possible for higher plants to grow there.

Some years ago, a volcano on the Indonesian island of Krakatau erupted. Not a plant or animal survived the rush of blistering-hot lava . . . or so it seemed. Time passed and the lava gradually cooled. The island still stood, a barren ugly rock, covered with cinders. And then about three years after the eruption of the volcano, natives venturing back to explore noticed a slimy green layer of algae on the rock. They thought it made the island even uglier. They did not know that the future of the island lay in the power of the cells of the tiny algae.

These little green plants multiplied and spread over the land. Seeds blew to the island from the mainland as they had been doing all along. But until the algae took

hold, the seeds died or were blown away again. It was only when the algae had been given enough time to enrich the soil that the seeds were able to take root. In a few years, the island was covered with lush tropical vegetation. It had been given a second chance at life by the algae.

The same sort of thing can happen to land that has

always been dismissed as too poor to bear crops. There were dry desert areas of India where for centuries nothing had grown. And then came the discovery of what algae could do. During the rainy season, blue-green algae were taken to the puddles and left there to grow. They improved the land so much that it can now be used for farming.

"There's nothing new about using algae as a soil conditioner," algologists insist. "Through the ages, primitive peoples have used seaweed as a simple fertilizer."

Nowadays we know that the microscopic blue-green algae are even better at the job. Dr. Mary Belle Allen, a leading chemist at the University of California, tried an experiment in her laboratory. She grew rice plants in glass beakers. Dr. Allen slipped some blue-green algae of a species called *anabaena cylindrica* into some of them; the others contained only sand and water. The rice plants surrounded by algae grew beautifully; the others soon died.

What was the secret? It lies in the chemistry of plants.

"If you analyze any rich soil where plants flourish," botanists explain, "you find that it contains a great deal of nitrogen. This has been known for a long time. And so when farmers try to improve soil, they add fertilizers which have a lot of nitrogen in them.

"Now algae can take nitrogen from the air and fix it in the soil where it is taken in by rice, grass, corn, wheat and other higher plants."

That is why the rice plants in the beakers with algae flourished. The others died as soon as they had used up the nitrogen in the sand. Rice cannot take nitrogen from the air the way algae can.

From the laboratory, scientists moved onto the land. Farmers used to turn up their noses at algae. They thought

The rice plant surrounded
by algae grew beautifully;
the other soon died.

them dirty and harmful until they learned that these tiny unappealing blue-green cells are plant lifesavers. Dr. Allen found that 480 pounds of nitrogen fertilizer would have to be added to each acre of land every month in order to get what comes naturally with algae.

As algae grow best in water, they are most useful in improving water crops. The most important of these is rice. If you have ever seen pictures of Chinese or Japanese rice fields, you know that rice grows in puddles, known as paddy fields. One scientist reported that four years after algae were added, rice fields yielded 128 per cent more rice than did those without algae. As rice is the basic food in Japan, China and most of the Far East, algae can mean a great deal to the vast population of those areas.

Rice was one of the very first crops cultivated by man, and so it seems fitting for the most primitive plant on earth to help it grow. But algae have an uncanny way of fitting into the world of the future. In our atomic age, the release of too much radioactivity is a great worry to thinking men everywhere. When you hear people discussing the dangers of nuclear testing, one of the things that concerns them is the amount of strontium 90 and other radioactive materials that fall out whenever there is an atomic blast. This fallout causes serious illnesses and produces physical defects in men and animals.

Once radioactivity is released, there is no way to get rid of it. The materials take a certain length of time to die, and no one can speed up that time or change it in any way.

You may be wondering what algae have to do with all this. These tiny plants offer us a hope of controlling at least a little of the radioactivity. The algae on the rocks of streams or the sides of reservoirs can absorb radioactivity from the water, leaving it fresh and pure. The radioactive materials still exist; they will decay in their own good time. But they are in a different place — in the algae cells. This is preferable in every way. We don't want radioactive materials in our bones, taken into our systems through our drinking water. We are quite ready to let algae have them.

And so algae not only bring us many good things, these tiny plants can also save us from harm.

11 ·

CONCLUSION: THE AGE OF ALGAE

"THEY USED to call us cranks," a noted algologist commented, smiling. "It wasn't too long ago either."

Until recently, algae were only considered suitable for botanical research into the process of photosynthesis. Anyone who suggested that they might have any general use as a food was immediately dismissed as peculiar.

No one denied that algae contained protein and vitamins. But what if they did? Even if you could eat algae, who would want to? It was one of those wild, impractical ideas, like living on dandelions or raw herbs. In time of war, it might be worth looking into. After all, ways of transforming sawdust into bread were studied during World War II. But when any other food at all is available, algae seem pretty unwholesome.

Scientists interested in algae as everyday food found their only allies among the government officials of crowded countries where people were starving. But the process of producing food from algae was so difficult and expensive that most of them threw up their hands in despair.

Algae might find some uses in the distant future, economists summed it up. If a time were to come when all natural resources were used up and everyone was starving, then — and only then — might algae replace corn, wheat, beef, and even coal and oil.

Just a few short years ago, even the staunchest supporters of algae were becoming discouraged.

"I'm ready to give up," said one of America's leading algologists in despair.

And then came the launching of the satellite Sputnik, and the space age was born. All at once, plans for travel to the moon, to Mars and Venus left the realm of science fiction and appeared on the pages of the daily newspapers. Blueprints of spaceships sped from the drawing boards of engineers. Fuels to get rockets off the ground were made by the big chemical companies. Astronomers mapped routes through the solar system. And biologists were handed the problem of how to keep men alive in space.

Algae became the plants of the hour. They could provide men with oxygen and food, use up their carbon dioxide and wastes. And they could keep on doing this indefinitely, as the spacemen pushed back the boundaries of the universe. Money was poured into algal research. Scientists were put to work by the Air Force, the Navy, the universities. They were encouraged to work harder and faster — to discover new strains of algae, new methods for using them as sources of oxygen and food.

All this excitement about algae brought side effects. Overpopulated countries began to take a second look at the tiny green plants. Maybe food could be made from them, after all. In highly developed nations, scientists began to look for industrial uses for algae. Gradually, the many possibilities are being explored.

These primitive plants are coming into their own in the space age. And what lies ahead?

A time may be coming when men will eat algae steaks and drink algae Cokes. They will heat their houses with algae. Air conditioners, washing machines and toasters will run on algal current. At ball games, algal power will keep the floodlights burning. When people are sick, they will be treated with medicines made of algae.

The ugly duckling of the stagnant ponds is slowly but surely turning into a swan.

INDEX